Union Pacific Rail Road

Across the Continent

West from Omaha, Nebraska.

1865 1870

OFFICERS OF THE COMPANY.

OLIVER AMES, PRESIDENT.
THOMAS C. DURANT, VICE-PRESIDENT.
JOHN J. CISCO, TREASURER.
CHARLES TUTTLE, ASSISTANT TREASURER.
HENRY B. HAMMOND, SECRETARY.

DIRECTORS.

OLIVER AMES, . . . Mass.
THOMAS C. DURANT, New York.
JOHN J. CISCO, . New York.
H. S. McCOMB, . . Delaware.
SIDNEY DILLON, . New York.
CORNELIUS S. BUSHNELL, Conn.
BENJAMIN E. BATES, . Mass.

JOHN DUFF, . . Mass.
JOSIAH BARDWELL, . Mass.
JOHN B. ALLEY, . . Mass.
EBENEZER COOK, . . Iowa.
F. GORDON DEXTER, . Mass.
CHAS. A. LAMBARD, . Mass.
WM. H. MACY, . . New York.

JOHN F. TRACY, Illinois.

GOVERNMENT DIRECTORS.

GEORGE ASHMAN, Massachusetts.
JESSE L. WILLIAMS, Indiana.
SAMUEL McKEE, Pennsylvania.
JAMES S. ROLLINS, Missouri.
JAMES BROOKS, New York.

TRUSTEES FOR THE BONDHOLDERS.

HON. E. D. MORGAN, New York.   HON. OAKES AMES, Mass.

GOVERNMENT COMMISSIONERS.

MAJ. WILLIAM M. WHITE, Connecticut.
GEN. FRANK P. BLAIR, Missouri.
GEN. JOHN BUFORD, Illinois.

GEN. G. M. DODGE, CHIEF ENGINEER.
COL. SILAS SEYMOUR, CONSULTING ENGINEER.

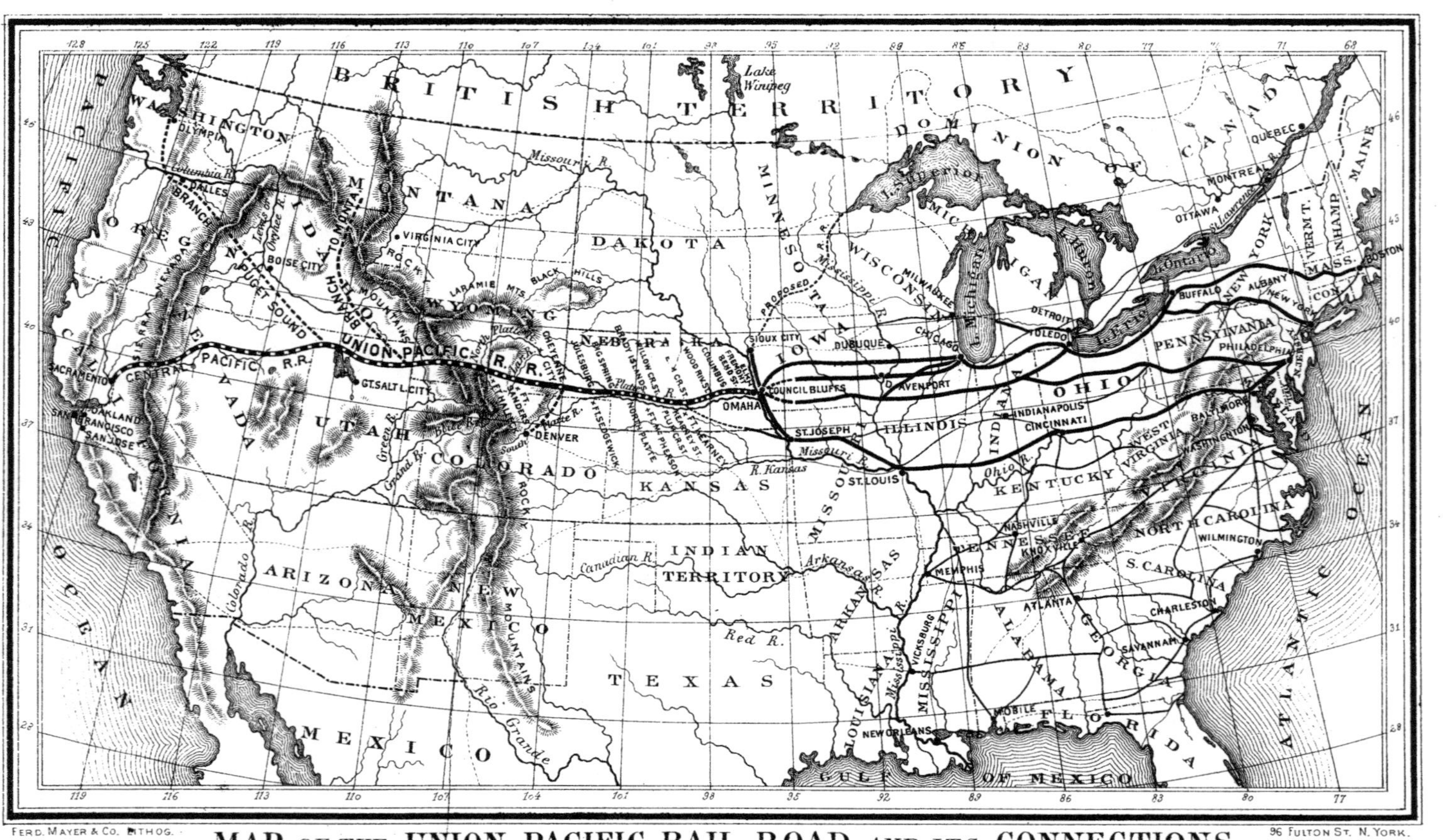

MAP OF THE UNION PACIFIC RAIL ROAD AND ITS CONNECTIONS.

THE

UNION PACIFIC RAILROAD

COMPANY,

CHARTERED BY THE UNITED STATES.

Progress of their Road

WEST FROM OMAHA, NEBRASKA,

ACROSS THE CONTINENT.

MAKING, WITH ITS CONNECTIONS, AN UNBROKEN LINE FROM THE ATLANTIC TO THE PACIFIC OCEAN.

FIVE HUNDRED AND FORTY MILES COMPLETED DECEMBER, 1867.

OFFICES,

No. 20 Nassau Street, New York.

New York:

PUBLISHED BY THE COMPANY.

[Pamphlet Edition, April 2, 1868.]

C. A. Alvord, Printer, 15 Vandewater Street.

Contents.

Introduction.

The Union Pacific Railroad a National Undertaking.

Beyond the western banks of the Mississippi and Missouri are more than two million square miles of the American Union. In 1860, less than half that area, east of these rivers, contained more than twenty-seven millions of people. The far western states and territories possess an amount of mineral wealth that is not even approached in any other country on the globe, and a large portion of their surface produces the most luxuriant and valuable crops. California, the Rocky Mountains, and the Sierra Nevadas, have already given us over twelve hundred million dollars in gold and silver, and are still giving us seventy-five millions a year. Large as these sums are, they only indicate what we should receive with improved facilities for transportation and internal development.

It is now twenty years since Col. Thomas H. Benton, the distinguished Senator from Missouri, introduced a bill to the United States Senate for the construction of a road to be of iron *where practicable* from the Mississippi river to the Pacific ocean. At that time, the difficulties in the way of building a *railroad* across the Rocky Mountains were thought too great to be surmounted, even with the help of an unencumbered national treasury, and the Senator's humbler project failed for want of support. But then, the Pacific coast was a wilderness, dotted only here and there with fur-traders' posts, and had no attractions for a resident population. Now, it is divided into powerful states, with large towns and cities, and contains nearly a million of inhabitants, who are actively engaged in all departments of production and traffic.

The Pacific coast has attained its present position against the most adverse circumstances. Immigration could reach it only by tedious and expensive sea-voyages by Cape Horn or Panama, or a still more protracted and painful journey of several months' duration across a dangerous wilderness. The time has certainly arrived when this western half of our great domain not only imperatively needs, but can abundantly sustain railroad communication. The beginning of the late civil war demonstrated its political as well as physical necessity. The Pacific States were practically thrice as distant from the Atlantic as Great Britain, and could take no part in the common cause, while in the event of foreign war, they would be especially exposed to attack without the possibility of receiving immediate aid. The propriety of establishing an independent Pacific Empire was openly discussed, and it was evident, that the unity and harmony of the country demanded that its distant parts should be brought more closely together.

Opening a vast territory to settlement would attract immigration, and its consequent production, and this would increase the general wealth, and lighten our taxes by a wider distribution. The improvement of one portion of a country or even of an estate, although at some first cost to other portions, soon benefits and enriches the whole. One great immediate result to be secured was the development of the vast mineral resources that were abundant along not less than a thousand miles of the proposed railroad line. California was rich in the precious metals, but other and less accessible regions were known to be richer. The cost of transporting the necessary mining machinery and means of subsistence by wagons across the plains, was $500 a ton, and as other incidental expenses were quite as great, only the richest veins of ore could be profitably worked. We were in debt, and nothing was so good to pay with as gold and silver. Indian wars were imminent, and there were no peacemakers or civilizers so cheap and so potent as the rail-track and the locomotive.

But how should this great national railroad be built? It must extend nearly sixteen hundred miles from the Missouri river, across the Great Plains, and over the successive and comparatively unexplored Rocky Mountain ranges, from Salt Lake down the Humboldt valley, and over and through the gigantic Sierra Nevadas until, within a hundred miles of Sacramento, it would reach the Pacific slope. Until this slope should be reached, the country was a wilderness, with but scanty facilities for railroad building, and with unknown, and therefore magnified, difficulties in the way. The lowest estimate for construction was more than one hundred million dollars, and it is not surprising that the boldest and most adventurous capitalists refused to furnish so large a sum for an enterprise whose importance but few seemed to appreciate, and in which fewer yet were willing to risk their money.

There was no alternative left but for the Government to execute or guarantee the work; but as public works are generally constructed, time and money would both be saved by throwing it open to competition. The Government therefore determined to give its aid in the most guarded manner to such responsible parties as were willing to invest a portion of their own means in the undertaking. To secure the greatest energy and efficiency, this aid was given to two powerful companies, viz., to THE UNION PACIFIC RAILROAD COMPANY, building from Omaha, on the Missouri river, *West;* and to THE CENTRAL PACIFIC RAILROAD COMPANY of California, building from Sacramento, *East,* until the two roads shall meet. The amount of aid given to each was made dependent upon the length of road each should build, and therefore each company is prompted to great efforts to secure the construction and control of the longest portion of what, when completed, will be ONE, AND THE ONLY GRAND RAILROAD LINE CONNECTING THE ATLANTIC AND PACIFIC COASTS.

Formation of the Union Pacific Railroad and Telegraph Company.

The preliminary organization of the Company was made in October, 1863; subscriptions were solicited from prominent capitalists, which at first were reluctantly made. At length, several hundred subscribers were obtained in various cities, a board of directors was chosen, and the Company was duly organized under the several Acts of Congress, approved by ABRAHAM LINCOLN, President of the United States, July 1 and July 12, 1862, and July 2, 1864, all of whose conditions have been complied with.*

There are fifteen directors on the part of the Company, and five directors appointed by the President of the United States to represent the Government. The authorized capital is One Hundred Million Dollars, of which $8,950,000 have been paid in by the stockholders upon the work already done. Additional amounts will be paid whenever the wants of the Company may demand; but it is not supposed that more than twenty-five millions will be necessary, and perhaps a considerably smaller sum will be sufficient.

*The various Congressional Acts and their amendments are too long to be recited here, but copies will be furnished free on application in person, or by mail, at the Company's offices, No. 20 Nassau Street, New York.

Progress of the Work.

Topography, Character of the Country, and Distances along the Line.

Numerous surveys for the purpose of determining the feasibility of a railroad to the Pacific, were made subsequent to the discovery of gold in California. In 1855, Gen. Greenville M. Dodge, now Chief Engineer of the road, thoroughly explored the several lines of approach to the Rocky Mountains from the Missouri, and obtained information which has been of great service in the final location of the work. The eastern portion of the route now occupied by the road—up the valley of the Platte—was the one over which the overland stages and much other overland travel passed, and was found to have special advantages of wood and water, and moderate grades.

The popular impression that the building of the Pacific Railroad, though physically practicable, required enormous expenditures of time and money, has been proved erroneous. The first contract for construction was made in August, 1864; but various conflicting interests, connected with the location of the line, delayed its progress, and the first forty miles were not laid until January, 1866. Since that time, the road has been built more rapidly than any similar work in the world. On the first of January, 1867, 305 miles were finished; now, 540 miles are in operation, and 100 miles more are ready for the iron.

Gen. Dodge furnishes the following notes on the general features of the country along the line west to Salt Lake: He says that the initial point of the Union Pacific, at Omaha, is 967 feet above tidewater; and Cheyenne, at the eastern base of the Laramie Range of the Rocky Mountains, 517 miles west from Omaha, is 6,062 feet. The difference in elevation between Omaha and Cheyenne is there-

fore 5,095 feet, or an average of about ten feet to the mile. Between these points, the line follows the comparatively level valleys of the Platte River and Lodge-Pole Creek, and requires but few important bridges. The summit of the Laramie Mountains, *the highest point on the line*, is 32 miles from Cheyenne, and its elevation is 8,262 feet, which leaves 2,200 feet to be overcome, at a maximum grade of 80 feet to the mile, which is much less formidable than the grades of many eastern roads.

There is no gorge at the summit, but a level plateau, which affords ample room for the necessary stations, turn-outs, etc. Dale Creek Cañon is crossed four miles from the summit, by a bridge 460 feet long, built upon nine piers, the highest being 125 feet. This will be the most important and expensive bridge on the route, but its cost will be very small compared with that of the Portage Bridge over the Genesee (N. Y.) River, which is 234 feet high and 800 feet long, built by Col. S. Seymour, now Consulting Engineer of the Union Pacific Railroad. From the summit to the Laramie Plains is 13 miles, with no grade more than 90 feet to the mile. It is 19 miles further to the Great Laramie River, which is spanned by a bridge 300 feet long and 16 feet above the water. From the Great Laramie to the Little Laramie, crossed by a bridge 250 feet long, is 15 miles; thence to Rock Creek is 30 miles, over an undulating country, with maximum grades not exceeding 40 feet to the mile. From Rock Creek to the Medicine Bow River is 28 miles, comprising a small amount of rock and excavation, but no cut more than 22 feet deep will be required. The Medicine Bow is crossed near the mouth of Rock Creek (93 miles west of the summit and 632 miles west of Omaha), and its valley is followed for eight miles, to the east range of the Rattlesnake Hills. The summit of these hills is reached at Brown's Pass (latitude 41.50, elevation 7,124 feet above the sea,) by following the valley and slopes of a tributary of the Medicine Bow, and descending from the summit west, the South Fork of the Platte is reached by a tributary of that stream known as Mary's Creek. The ascent to the Pass is made with no grade exceeding 65 feet to the mile, and the descent to the North Fork of the Platte with no grade exceeding 50 feet. In descending to the North Fork, the line passes the western range of the Rattlesnake Hills, through one of the characteristic cañons of the Rocky Mountains, and thus avoids the steep inclines incident to most mountain regions. The road crosses the North Fork of the Platte River by a 650 feet Howe truss bridge, at an elevation of 6,484 feet above the sea;—distance from Omaha, 691 miles.

From this point, the road takes about a due west course, and begins to ascend the main divide of the continent. It follows a succession of basins or depressions in the country, which are independent in themselves, and which are drained entirely by evaporation and underground communication. The road passes Rawlins' Springs, Duff's Peak and Separation Creek, and reaches the divide of the Continent at Dodge's Pass, 51 miles west of the North Fork of the Platte, and 725 miles west of Omaha, at an elevation of 7,108 feet above the sea.* This main divide is a broad open plain, extending from the snowy mountain ranges on the south, near Bridger's Pass, to the South Pass, near the southerly point of the Wind River Mountains, and supports a luxuriant growth of grass. The maximum grade in ascending this divide is but 65 feet to the mile, and the line then descends, at a maximum grade of 60 feet, into Dodge's Basin, passing Clay and Steamboat Buttes. It rises from this point to the west rim of Dodge's Basin, and descends to Bitter Creek, at Big Pond Station, and follows the Bitter Creek Valley 61 miles to Green River, 841 miles west of Omaha. Green River is 6,092 feet above the sea, and is crossed by a bridge 650 feet long. From this point, the line crosses to Black's Fork of Green River, extending along a fine, wide valley, to the mouth of the Big Muddy, which it follows to the east rim of the Great Salt Lake Basin. We ascend this rim on the slope of one of the tributaries of the Big Muddy, and follow a continuous ridge until we reach a summit 7,567 feet above the sea. From this point, we descend gradually to Bear River, and up Yellow Creek to the Wahsatch Moun-

*The reader should remember that the *base* of the Rocky Mountains at Cheyenne is 6,062 feet above the sea, and that the engineering difficulties to be overcome begin at that elevation, and are therefore much less formidable in reality than they appear on paper.

tains, 6,879 feet above the sea, and then descend rapidly—piercing a ridge by a tunnel 700 feet long—to the valley of Echo Cañon, which is followed down to the Weber valley, where we run through the cultivated farms of the Mormons. Following the cañons through a range of the Wahsatch seven miles, with three short tunnels, near the mouth of Lost Creek—called "The Narrows"—we come out upon the broad table-lands of the Weber Valley, and soon strike Great Salt Lake Valley at the mouth of the Weber Cañon. From here, we skirt the Great Salt Lake 35 miles, to near Great Salt Lake City, 214 miles from Green River, 1,037 miles west from Omaha, and 4,245 feet above the sea level.

It is worthy of note that the line of the Union Pacific Railroad has no grades over 90 feet to the mile, and then only for very short distances, while the grade of the Baltimore & Ohio Railroad is 116 feet to the mile for 19 miles, and the Virginia Central Railroad crosses the Blue Ridge on an incline of 250 feet to the mile.

The following table shows the distance from the eastern terminus of the road to the prominent points along the line, with their elevation above the sea level:

STATION.	DISTANCE FROM OMAHA.	ELEVATION ABOVE THE SEA.
Omaha,	— miles.	967 feet.
Fremont,	46 "	1,215 "
Columbus,	91 "	1,455 "
Kearney,	190 "	2,128 "
North Platte,	290 "	2,830 "
Julesburg,	377 "	3,557 "
Cheyenne,	517 "	6,062 "
Evans' Pass, Summit of Black Hills,	550 "	8,262 "
Laramie River,	576 "	7,134 "
Bridger's Pass, Rocky Mountains,	690 "	7,534 "
Green River,	820 "	6,092 "
Fort Bridger,	845 "	7,009 "
Weber Canon,	995 "	4,654 "
Humboldt Wells,	1,213 "	5,650 "
Humboldt Lake,	1,493 "	4,047 "
Big Bend Truckee,	1,534 "	4,217 "
Truckee River,	1,602 "	5,866 "
Summit of Sierras,	1,616 "	7,042 "
Cisco,	1,624 "	5,711 "
Alta,	1,652 "	3,625 "
Colfax,	1,667 "	2,448 "
Sacramento,	1,721 "	56 "
Stockton,	1,766 "	22 "
San Francisco,	1,845 "	—

Agricultural Resources, Timber, Minerals, &c.

Farming and Grazing Lands.

The lands for two hundred miles west of the Missouri river belonging to the Company which are now surveyed, amounting to two millions of acres, are susceptible of the highest cultivation, and will be sold at low prices, and on favorable terms of payment.* They are mostly in the Platte valley—every foot of them subject to tillage, are well watered, well drained, and the soil is very rich. The lands extending from Fort Kearney to the eastern base of the mountains require irrigation to secure crops, but they are covered with a growth of buffalo and bunch grasses at all seasons of the year, and afford the finest pasturage in the world. At the base of the mountains, and along the valleys of all the water-courses heading in the granite formations, the lands are good, and well adapted to settlement, and the valleys of the mountain streams of Colorado to-day afford a better recompense to the farmer than any gold mine in that Territory.

The lands on the Laramie Plains are high, but are mostly well watered, and vegetables, small grains, &c., thrive well. The valleys of Green River, Black Fork, and the streams east of the rim of the great basin are from one to five miles wide, well watered, and will support a large population. The valleys of the Weber River and Great Salt Lake are already thickly settled, and yield immense crops of grain and vegetables, while for fruit, they are perhaps unequalled in the United States. While it is true that a portion of the Company's land among the Rocky Mountains is not very valuable for agricultural purposes, there can be no doubt that another large proportion is unsurpassed for fertility, and other portions are rich in timber, coal, iron, and the precious metals.

* It is expected that full particulars in relation to these lands will be printed and ready for circulation in May, when the Company will be pleased to respond to letters of inquiry.

Silver and Gold.

The mines of Colorado that will receive all their supplies and transport all their exports over this road, are so well known as to need no explanation here. The new mines lately discovered at the head of the Sweet Water, and along the east base of the Wind River Mountains, are all tributary to it. So far as developed, these mines are as rich as any yet known, and no doubt the country in the north from the Big Horn mountains to Green River is rich in the precious metals. The heads of the Powder River, the different tributaries of the Platte and Sweet Water, the immense country drained by the tributaries of the Big Horn River, Wind River, Porpogie and Sweet Water are already being prospected, and quartz lodes and placer mines are being discovered over all that vast extent of country. No man can now predict the amount of trade, travel, and traffic these mines will build up for the road.

In the report of the Commissioner of Mining Statistics, J. Ross Browne, recently submitted to Congress by the Secretary of the Treasury, the mineral yield of the States and Territories for 1867, is estimated as follows:

California,	$25,000,000	Colorado,	2,500,000
Nevada,	20,000,000	New-Mexico,	500,000
Montana,	12,000,000	Arizona,	500,000
Idaho,	6,500,000	Miscellaneous,	5,000,000
Washington,	1,000,000		
Oregon,	2,000,000	Total,	$75,000,000

The entire product of the precious metals from 1848 to Jan. 1, 1868, is estimated as follows:

California,	$900,000,000	Colorado,	25,000,000
Montana,	65,000,000	New Mexico and Arizona	5,000,000
Nevada,	90,000,000	Miscellaneous	45,000,000
Idaho,	45,000,000	Retained for plate, jewelry, etc.	50,000,000
Washington,	10,000,000		
Oregon,	20,000,000	Total,	$1,255,000,000

Mr. Browne says of the region under consideration: "The area of land suitable for cultivation is much larger than was originally supposed, and important results are anticipated from the completion of the Pacific Railroad.

Timber.

Pine, Spruce and Hemlock grow on the Black Hills in large quantities, and skirt the mountains to the south for 300 miles. The immense forests on the Medicine Bow, Elk, and other mountain ranges are inexhaustible, and the great streams, the Laramies, Medicine Bow, and North Platte, that rise among them, furnish easy transportation by rafts to bring their products to the Union Pacific road. West of the main divide on the heads of Green River, New Fork, Piney, and Labarge, on the north, and Black Fork, Henry's Fork, Bear River and Weber on the south, are some of the finest Pine forests in the country; they are hundreds of miles in extent, and are capable of being brought to this road by the streams above mentioned, which are in good rafting condition during the Spring.

Coal.

The best Coal yet discovered near the line is situated about 500 miles west of the Missouri river, and extends south along the Denver Branch to Colorado, and has been used by the people of that State for years. The veins run from two feet to sixteen feet in thickness, have good floors and excellent slate roofs, and are easily and cheaply mined. Crossing the Laramie range of mountains and striking the Laramie Plains, the railroad immediately enters the great coal field of that country and runs directly through it for over four hundred miles. This coal region has not been fully developed, but no doubt exists that it is the finest coal field west of the Missouri river. The veins run from two to twenty feet in thickness, and are easy of access, often lying above the grade of the road, and have a dip that makes them cheaply and easily drained, while the supply for all time to come is inexhaustible. After crossing the Wahsatch range of mountains, coal is again found along Weber valley sufficient for all practical purposes.

Iron.

Limonite and Hemitite ores are found in vast quantities at the eastern base of the mountains on the Laramie Plains, and in portions of the Great Salt Lake Basin. Mountains of magnetic ore have been discovered on the Chugwater, easy of access from the line, and also on the north fork of the Platte. On the Weber River, iron ore exists in inexhaustible quantities, and so far as tested it is equal in quality to the average found anywhere in the United States.

Mineral Springs.

Along the Wahsatch Mountains and the valley of the Wind River, and the forks of the Porpogies, oil springs have been found, and some of them are already producing coal oil for lubricating and illuminating purposes. The salt and mineral springs along the line are the finest in the country,—the salt springs being so strong that five buckets of the water will make one bucket of salt. The mineral waters have remarkable medicinal qualities, and the soda springs of Bear River are believed to be the purest yet known.

How the Union Pacific Railroad is Built.

The advance of the builders is like that of a great army, rather than like that of men engaged in ordinary industry. Topographical parties, fully armed and equipped, were out like scouts, for two or three years, carefully examining the country in all directions, to determine the most favorable route. The engineers followed, like skirmishers in the advance, to drive the stakes and lay out the long line on which that great prize, the trade of China and the Indies, was to be contended for. Then came the companies, regiments, and divisions of sturdy laborers, armed with pickaxes and shovels, which, peaceful as they are, have conquered and held a great deal more of the earth than muskets and bayonets. They are followed by the graders and mechanics, the track-layers, &c., supported by squadrons of horse and trains of wagons, that stretch for many miles across the plains. The sub-contractors work in sections of about two miles each, and pitch their white tents in military style. From 50 to 500 men work in each section, and make the road-bed ready for the track-layers. A much larger force will be employed upon the Union Pacific Railroad during 1868 than ever before. Rock-cuttings have been continued in the Laramie Mountains during the entire winter, and there has been much less snow there, than in the latitude of New York city. Not less than 8,000 additional laborers will be in the field this season, besides 1,000 mechanics, bridge builders, iron workers, &c. There will also be 2,000 teams, with the necessary horses and mules for the plows and scrapers, and not less than 1,500 wagons and carts. Much of the lumber for bridges, ties, &c., is already cut, and saw-mills and shops are busy in turning out the mechanical appliances for the great work. Iron sufficient to lay 200 miles of track has already been delivered on the ground, and there is every prospect that not less than 300 miles more road will be finished during the present year.

An intelligent correspondent of the *Cincinnati Gazette,* who traveled over the portion of road that was completed in June, 1867, has written a very interesting letter, showing in detail the manner in which the work is done. He says:

"There is nothing connected with the Union Pacific Railroad that is not wonderful. In one sense the road is as great an achievement as the war, and as grand a triumph. One year ago, but forty miles were finished; this morning, we look back from our train over a day's rapid run, and forward sixty miles. Our party left the depot at Omaha at 9 o'clock on the morning of the 3d inst. The station-house, and the common passenger cars, were better than those on the road from Washington to New York. The train, which was made up for the excursionists, consisted of cars as elegant as any that can be found east of the Missouri.

Valley of the Platte.

"Long before the valley is reached, it spreads before the eye like a vast bay opening out into an ocean, whither the track appears to lead. It is forty miles from the low, rolling hills on the north, to the opposite and similar range on the south. Between, the surface is almost perfectly flat, though its regular ascent toward the west, of about ten feet to the mile, gives ample drainage. The soil is very rich, and the mind falters in its attempt to estimate the future of such a valley, or its immense capabilities. The grain fields of Europe are mere garden patches beside the green oceans which roll from Colorado to Indiana. The valley widens with the advance. The hills behind sink into the plain until the horizon there is perfect.

"Much of the land at the mouth of the valley is under cultivation, and the deep black of the freshly turned loam, the dark green of the wheat, the lighter grass, the deeper shades, and the brown of that which the fires of the autumn spared, make up the wide expanse a mosaic which nature alone could color, and the prairies only find room to display. Further on, huge plows, drawn by eight oxen, labored slowly along, each furrow being an added ripple to the tide which is sweeping up over all these rich regions—a tide whose ebb the youngest will never know.

A Frontier City.

"Crossing the North Platte, on a bridge about three thousand feet long, the train soon stopped at North Platte Station. Last fall there was no building here. Now the railroad company have fine brick car houses, there is a good hotel, where excellent fare is provided, and on the main street fronting the track are thirty-six buildings.

"Three hundred and twenty-five miles out, a construction train of eighty cars stood on a side track. It was loaded with iron, ties, spikes, and chairs, in exactly such proportions as were needed. It looked the very embodiment of system, and was one key to the rapidity with which the work progresses. A little farther on stood a similar train, and next we stopped in rear of the one where the track-layers resided.

"The road had been a constant wonder from the start. Its depots, its car-shops, its equipment, its remarkable smoothness, its high rate of speed, its long bridges, and its well ordered eating-houses, had attracted constant attention to it as a railroad alone. Every step trod revealed new wonders. The great achievement grew upward toward its real proportions with every throb of the engine. But all we saw was commonplace and natural beside the scene that awaited us where the track was being laid. If the rest had excited amazement, this new wonder took all the attributes of magic. Fictions of the East must be re-written to match the realities of this West.

The Track-Layers.

"The plain facts will reveal the magnitude of the work. There is really little known by the people of the character of the enterprise. Most think that a company of capitalists are hastily putting down a rude track, over which cars can be moved with care, for the purpose of securing lands and money from the Government. The fact is that one of the most complete roads of which the country can boast, with equipments that surpass many, is being laid with a speed that fails to impress the nation simply because it is not believed. But let the facts tell their plain yet wonderful story.

"Go back twenty miles on the road, and look at the immense construction trains, loaded with ties and rails, and all things needed for the work. It is like the grand reserve of an army. Six miles back are other trains of like character. These are the second line. Next, near the terminus, and following it hour by hour, are the boarding cars and a construction train, which answer to the actual battle line. The one is the camp; the other is the ammunition used in the fight. The boarding cars are each eighty feet long. Some are fitted with berths; two are dining halls; one is a kitchen, store-room and office.

"The boarding cars go in advance. They are pushed to the extremity of the track; a construction train then runs up, unloads its material and starts back to bring another from the second line. The boarding train is then run back till it has cleared the unloaded material. The trucks, each drawn by two horses, ply between the track-layers and their supplies. One of these trucks takes on a load of rails, about forty, with the proper proportion of spikes and chairs, making a load, when the horses are started off on a full gallop for the track-layers. On each side of these trucks are rollers to facilitate running off the iron.

"The rails within reach, parties of five men stand on either side. One in the rear throws a rail upon the rollers, three in advance seize it, and run out with it to the proper distance. The chairs have, meantime, been set under the last rails placed. The two men in the rear, with a single swing, force the end of the rail into the chair, and the chief of the squad calls out 'Down,' in a tone that equals the 'Forward' to any army. Every thirty seconds there came that brave 'Down,' 'Down,' on either side the track. They were the pendulum beats of a mighty era; they marked the time of the march and its regulation beat."

Branch and Connecting Roads.

The Idaho, Oregon & Puget's Sound—The Branch to Montana—The Denver, and Central Pacific.

While the construction of the main line of the Union Pacific Railroad is of paramount importance, the building of branch and connecting railroads is also a work of magnitude and of great value. Branch roads to Colorado, Oregon and Montana are projected. Arapahoe county, Colorado, by a vote of 1,210 for to 15 against, on the 20th of January, 1868, decided to take $500,000 of the stock of a railroad connecting Denver with the Union Pacific road, in the vicinity of Cheyenne, a distance of 100 miles, and that road will doubtless soon be built.

A bill has been introduced into Congress to incorporate the Idaho, Oregon & Puget's Sound Railroad Company, which contemplates not only a road to the points indicated in the company title, but also a branch to Montana. The report of the chief engineer of the company upon the Oregon route, says that to reach the navigable waters of the Pacific by the Snake River route will require the construction of but 400 miles of additional road, and this through a country abounding in timber and coal, and capable of sustaining a large population. The road could be built at the rate of 300 miles per year, and in the words of the engineer, "the local business of Oregon and Idaho would support it to-day. No such difficulties in obtaining material, labor, or transportation would be encountered on this line as we have had to encounter in building the Union Pacific."

The Montana branch would leave the Oregon line in Snake River Valley, and, by a feasible route, would reach the heart of the Territory in a distance of 200 miles. By beginning active work in the spring of 1869, the fall of 1870 would give Montana, Idaho, Washington, and Oregon Territories direct steam communication with all points east, whereas, by the route to which they have been looking for railroad connection—the Northern Pacific—they would have to wait years for the building of 1,700 miles, instead of the 400 which are here necessary.

The eastern connection of the Union Pacific, by the way of the Chicago & Northwestern Railroad, is complete, and several other eastern railroads are now being extended to Omaha, which already contains 15,000 inhabitants, and is the center of a very large traffic. Indeed, the business of all the great eastern lines will necessarily converge to this point, and pass over the Union Pacific Railroad.

The Central Pacific of California, which will form the western or Pacific coast connection, is being pushed forward with great energy, and, beginning at Sacramento, has already crossed the Sierra Nevada Mountains, which were the most formidable barrier to be surmounted on the whole Pacific line. The Central Pacific company report that they have already expended twenty-one million dollars ($21,000,000), have nearly finished 150 miles, and that, as they will soon come upon the Truckee and Humboldt valleys, they have no doubt that they will be able to meet the Union Pacific in 1870.

Resources for Construction.

When Congress determined that the Pacific Railroad should be built with the aid of the Government, it also determined that that aid should be ample to accomplish the purpose. No half-way measures would answer. The most feasible route across the continent was selected, which should be the Grand Trunk Line—the western artery of the whole railroad system of the United States. The grants in aid of construction are as follows:

1st. THE RIGHTS OF WAY AND MATERIAL, which include all necessary public lands for track, stations, depots, timber, stone, &c.

2d. THE GRANT OF MONEY.—The Government grants its six per cent. currency interest thirty-year bonds to the Union Pacific Railroad, to the following amounts:

On the plain portion of the road, extending from Omaha to the base of the Rocky Mountains, 517 miles, at the rate of $16,000 per mile, is	$8,272,000
On the most difficult portion of the road, extending from the eastern base of the Rocky Mountains westwardly, 150 miles, at the rate of $48,000 per mile, is	7,200,000
On the remaining distance westwardly towards the California State line, at the rate of $32,000 per mile. Estimating the distance to be built by the Union Pacific Company, before meeting with the Central Pacific at 1,100 miles, this would leave a remainder of 433 miles, at $32,000 per mile, which is . .	13,856,000
Or a total, for 1,100 miles of	$29,328,000

These bonds are issued only on the completion of each section of twenty miles of road, and upon the certificate of commissioners appointed by the United States Government that the road is thoroughly built and adequately supplied with all the machinery, equipment and fixtures necessary to complete a first-class railroad. The interest on these bonds is paid by the U. S. Treasury, but is a charge against the Company, which is much more than reimbursed by services rendered the Government in transporting its troops, freight, mails, &c. By its charter, the Company receives one-half the amount of its charges against the Government in money, and the remaining half is placed to its credit as a sinking fund, which may amount to a sum sufficient to retire the Government bonds at maturity.

It should be remembered *that both divisions of the great Pacific line stand upon precisely the same footing in this and in all other particulars respecting the Government grants.* (See Acts of Congress.)

3d. THE GRANT OF LANDS.—The Government grants to the Company every alternate section of land for twenty miles on each side of the road, making in all *twenty sections,* equal to 12,800 acres for each mile of the railroad. For a distance of 1,100 miles, this grant, which is an absolute donation, amounts to fourteen million and eighty thousand (14,080,000) acres. As the railroad follows the rich valley of the Great Platte for nearly 300 miles, a large portion of these lands may be classed among the most productive in the world, and, indeed, there can hardly be any lands along the line of such an important road that will not command a reasonable price for tillage, grazing or timber. It will certainly be quite within bounds to estimate them at an average of $1.50 per acre, and competent experts value them at a much higher rate. On the 7th of March, 1868, the President of the United States signed a congressional bill which provides that the alternate sections of land belonging to the Government on the line of the Union Pacific Railroad shall not be sold at less than $2.50 per acre.

4th. THE LOAN GRANT.—The Government grants the Company a right to issue its own First Mortgage Bonds on its railroad and telegraph lines to an amount equal to that of the bonds of the United States issued to the Company. By special act of Congress [passed July 2, 1864], these First Mortgage Bonds *are made a lien prior to all claims of the Government, or to any claims whatsoever.*

This gives the Union Pacific Railroad Company the following resources, exclusive of its capital stock, for the construction of 1,100 miles of road:

U. S. Bonds on 517 miles at $16,000 per mile,	$8,272,000
" " 150 " 48,000 "	7,200,000
" " 433 " 32,000 "	13,856,000
	$29,328,000
The Company's own First Mortgage Bonds to same amount,	29,328,000
Land Grant of 12,800 acres per mile, at $1.50 per acre,	21,120,000
Total,	$79,776,000

The Means Sufficient to Build the Road.

The supposed great difficulties in the way of building the Pacific Railroad have diminished as they have been encountered. Contracts for the construction of 914 miles west from Omaha, comprising much of the most difficult mountain work, and embracing every expense except surveying, have been made with responsible parties (who have already finished 540 miles,) at the average rate of sixty-eight thousand and fifty-eight dollars ($68,058) per mile. This price includes all necessary car-shops, depots, stations, and all other incidental buildings, and also locomotives, passenger, baggage and freight cars, and other requisite rolling-stock, to an amount that shall not be less than $7,500 per mile. Allowing the cost of the remaining one hundred and eighty-six of the eleven hundred miles assumed to be built by the Union Pacific Company to be $90,000 per mile,

THE TOTAL COST OF ELEVEN HUNDRED MILES AND EQUIPMENT, WILL BE AS FOLLOWS:

914 miles, at $68,058,	$62,205,012
186 " 90,000,	16,740,000
Add interest and miscellaneous expenses, surveys, &c.,	3,500,000
Amount,	$82,445,012

As the U. S. Bonds are equal to money, and the Company's own First Mortgage Bonds have a ready market, we have as the

AVAILABLE CASH RESOURCES FOR BUILDING ELEVEN HUNDRED MILES,

U. S. Bonds, ...	$29,328,000
First Mortgage Bonds, ...	29,328,000
Capital stock paid in on the work now done, ...	8,950,000
Land Grant, 14,080,000 acres, at $1.50 per acre, ...	21,120,000
Total, ...	$88,726,000

The Company have ample facilities for supplying any deficiency that may arise in means for construction. This may be done wholly or in part by additional subscriptions to the stock, for the capital which was refused at the beginning of the enterprise, is now freely and abundantly offered as its security and profit are demonstrated.

Anticipated Business and Profits of the Company.

Hon. E. D. Mansfield, Commissioner of Statistics for the State of Ohio, and a gentleman believed to be more familiar with railroad enterprises in their relation to the development of the country than any other, makes the following estimates in relation to the prospects of this Company. He says:

"We have some authentic facts on which to base a fair estimate of the business of the Pacific Railroad, when it is completed. In a general view, we find the fact of an intermediate unsettled country counterbalanced by the millions of persons and tonnage of products on either side seeking mutual intercourse. On this point we have the following facts, derived from Shipping Lists, Insurance Companies, Railroads, and general information:

Ships going from the Atlantic around Cape Horn—100, . .	80,000 tons.
Steamships connecting at Panama with California and China—55,	120,000 "
Overland Trains, Stages, Horses, &c., ...	30,000 "

"Here we have two hundred and thirty thousand tons carried westward; and experience has shown, that in the last few years the returned passengers from California have been nearly as numerous as those going. So also the great mass of gold and silver flows eastward; latterly there is an importation of wheat from California and goods from China by the Pacific route. Fairly assuming, therefore, that the trade each way will be about equal, we have 460,000 tons as *the actual freight across the continent.*

"How many passengers are there? We make the following estimate:

110 (both ways) steamships,	50,000
200 " vessels,	4,000
Overland (both ways),	100,000
Number per annum,	154,000

"Present prices (averaging half the cost of the steamships), for both passengers and tonnage, give this result:

154,000 passengers at $100,	$15,400,000
460,000 tons rated at $1 per cubic foot,	15,640,000
Present Cost of Transportation,	$31,040,000

"There can be no doubt that the number of passengers will be more than doubled by the completion of the road; so also, the road would take all the very light and valuable goods, which would be greatly increased *by the China trade.* Taking these things into view—estimating passengers at 7½ cents per mile, and goods at $1 per cubic foot—we have

300,000 passengers at $150 each,	$45,000,000
300,000 tons at $34,	10,200,000
Gross receipts,	$55,200,000

"Suppose that the proportion accruing to the Union Pacific is $30,000,000, then estimate the running expenses at one-half, and this would leave a net profit of $15,000,000.

"This may seem very large to those who have not examined the subject, but it must be remembered—1st, that the longest lines of road are the most profitable; 2d, that this road connects two oceans, and the vast populations of Western Europe and Eastern Asia; 3d, that the immense mining regions of Idaho, Montana, Nevada, and California, just developing, will produce a transit of persons and freight, at present beyond belief. We leave this estimate on record as a moderate (not an exaggerated,) view of the business and profits which may be fairly expected from the Grand Pacific Railroad."

Estimates of *future* business are doubtless valuable and important, and it does not follow that they are always too large. When the New York & Erie Railroad was first projected, its future business was estimated by its friends at *three* millions per annum, while it is now *over fifteen* millions, and will steadily increase. In the first circular issued by the Union Pacific Railroad Company, (in May, 1867,) it was said: "Counting nothing upon the great increase of business with increased facilities, the forty million pounds of freight going over the 305 miles already completed would give a gross receipt of $1,000,000 per year." How far this estimate has been exceeded by the facts, is shown in the official statement that the freight earnings in *eight months,* ending December 31st, 1867, were almost two million dollars. It must be remembered that for many years to come this Union Pacific and its western connections will be the *only* Pacific Railroad, and, as it will be without competition, it can always charge remunerative prices.

The anticipation of the early completion of the Pacific Railroad has recently stimulated all kinds of productive industry in California to prepare for that means of rapid communication which is so soon to multiply her numbers and wealth in a greater ratio than ever. Factories are being erected, large flouring mills established, vineyards planted, and farms extended, that the state may be ready to receive the great tide of population that must soon flow into it over the Pacific Railroad. The East is also preparing to accommodate itself to the forthcoming changes in the current of business. The Pacific Mail Steamship Company of New York are now running a regular line of their splendid steamers between San Francisco and China and Japan, which is doubtless the pioneer of other lines, that will traverse the Pacific Ocean laden with the teas, spices, and other products of Eastern Asia. Excepting some very heavy or bulky articles, of comparatively low values, shortness of time decides the direction of freights, and most of these cargoes will find their natural transit over the Union Pacific Railroad.

While the Company have had great confidence in its prospective earnings, they have carefully abstained from expressing any opinions that might be thought exaggerated or unwarranted. It requires no argument to show that the through traffic on the completed line of the Pacific Railroad must be immense. Now, the population of the Pacific States and Territories can hardly be less than one million, which the road itself will be the means of doubling every few years. The region traversed will contain an unusual proportion of miners and traders, whose commercial pursuits will make them the most active travelers and freighters, and consequently the best customers of a railroad. The editor of *Harper's Weekly,* who has given this subject careful attention, says:

"When the Pacific Railroad is completed to San Francisco, a new era will be inaugurated. The road will then be the grand artery of the country. All other lines of railway will become, to a certain extent, its feeders. Along its entire route over the great plains lateral branches will be constructed to tap it, which will pour into it their wayside contributions to an extent that can not to-day be approximately estimated. The road will not supersede the California ships in carrying bulky freight to New York, but the 'way' traffic will undoubtedly be something marvelous. Already, with less than one-third of its length complete, it is earning four times its operating expenses, as officially stated. Such success is without precedent. When it reaches the already populous gold regions of Montana, Idaho, and Nevada, the freight to and from those points alone is likely to be something almost fabulous. And population follows the road as it extends. A town or village marks each stage of its progress. Who can calculate the quantity of way freight that the road is destined to carry for those growing communities—who, indeed, can estimate the passenger traffic alone? When hundreds of thousands of persons, with their faces toward the west, have tramped over the plains at the risk of their scalps, how many peradventure will ride when they can make the journey with safety in a few days? Then comes the natural inquiry whether a single track, with its infrequent sidings and turnouts, will be able to accommodate more than the mere passenger traffic of the road, or whether travelers to the Pacific will be content to abide a time-schedule adapted to slow-moving freight-trains as well as passenger express cars. Certainly but a short time will elapse before the demands of trade will call for a second track, to be used exclusively as a freight road, over which an endless line of slowly-moving vans shall continuously pass, leaving the other track for the use of impatient passengers only."

The Way Business—Actual Earnings.

As no one has ever expressed a doubt, that as soon as the road is completed, its through business will be abundantly profitable, it becomes interesting to know, not only what may be expected, but what has actually been earned, by the way, or local business, so far as it has been opened. It should be remembered that, although settlements are being rapidly made along the line, until recently the road has run through a wilderness for almost its entire length; but as every year brings an influx of population, this local traffic will have a steadily increasing value. At present, its transportation for the government and for the mining regions is the chief source of its already large revenue. As these mining regions are penetrated, the earnings will be greatly increased, and the various branch lines that will soon be constructed will be most valuable feeders of the main trunk. Mails and passengers have already been brought through from San Francisco, by the Union Pacific Railroad and Wells, Fargo & Co.'s stages, in fifteen days (the steamer requires twenty-one to twenty-four days), and, as the eastern and western ends of the track are brought nearer together, there can be no doubt that by next season, at least one-half of the California passenger travel will take this route. The distance intervening between the two railroads will be nothing but a pleasant episode in a most picturesque region, that will agreeably vary the monotony of railway travel, and must be more attractive than three to four weeks' confinement on board a steamer.

The road was run by the contractors until April, 1867, but its

Earnings from May 1st, 1867, to Dec. 31st, 1867,

a period of eight months, are officially reported as follows:

From Passengers,	$526,779 23
From Freight,	1,912,028 49
From Express,	17,886 05
Mails,	32,273 28
Miscellaneous,	7,223 29
Total,	$2,496,190 34

Expenses from May 1st, 1867, to Dec. 31st, 1867.

Conducting Transportation,	$282,022 23
Motive Power, Engines, &c.,	567,355 45
Maintenance of Way,	430,641 18
Maintenance of Cars,	91,208 30
General Expenses,	55,827 10
	$1,427,054 26
Net Earnings to Balance,	1,069,136 08
Total,	$2,496,190 34

The average length of road in operation for the eight months, from May 1st to December 31st, was 386 miles.

The amount of First Mortgage Bonds the Company can issue on 386 miles, at $16,000 per mile, is $6,176,000.

Gold Interest for eight months at the rate of 6 per cent.,	$247,040
Add 40 per cent. premium for Gold,	98,816
Total,	$345,856
Surplus after paying interest on First Mortgage Bonds,	$723,280

It will be seen that the net earnings have already been more than three times this interest.

We will now add to the account, the interest on the U. S. Second Mortgage Bonds, and it will stand as follows:

Net Earnings for eight months,		$1,069,136 08
Interest on First M. Bonds, reduced to currency,	$345,856	
" " Second " in currency,	247,040	
Total,		$592,896 00
Surplus after paying all interests,		$476,240 08

The amount paid by the Government for the transportation of troops, munitions, stores and mails has been, and doubtless will continue to be much more than the interest on the United States Second Mortgage Bonds. If it is not, the charter provides that after the road is completed, and until said bonds and interest are paid, at least five per cent. of the net earnings of the road shall be applied to such payment.

The statement of earnings would have been much larger, if the company had not thought it wise to facilitate the early completion of the work, by reducing the charges to contractors for transporting iron and other materials. It is doubtless better to sacrifice a present profit and the advantage of showing very large present earnings, to secure the greater gains and advantages that must accrue from reach-

ing the through traffic at the earliest practicable moment. At the time the act of incorporation was passed, it was expected that the earnings of the road would be very large, and the government reserved the right to reduce the Company's charges whenever the profit on the cost of the completed line should be more than ten per cent. per annum. [Sec. 18, act of 1862.]

The Union Pacific Railroad Company's First Mortgage Bonds.

Their Security and Value.

As before stated, the Union Pacific Railroad Company are authorized by Congress to issue their First Mortgage Bonds in the same amounts as are issued by the Government to the Company on the various sections of the road *as they are completed*, viz.:

On the first 517 miles at $16,000 per mile, . . .	$8,272,000
On Rocky Mountain region, 150 miles, at $48,000 per mile, -	7,200,000
On 433 additional miles at $32,000 per mile, . . .	13,856,000
Total for 1,100 miles, ...	$29,328,000

All these bonds are for $1,000 each, and have coupons attached. They have thirty years to run, and bear interest at the rate of six per cent. per annum *in gold,* payable on the first days of January and July, at the Company's Offices in the city of New York.

Principal as well as Interest Payable in Gold.

The recent agitation in relation to the redemption of the government bonds in currency, has induced many parties to inquire how the principal of the Union Pacific Bonds will be paid. While the Company have never supposed that it would be paid otherwise than in gold, yet, to put all question on this subject at rest, at a meeting of the directors held on the 12th of March, 1868, it was unanimously

Resolved, That the President and Treasurer are authorized and directed to enter into a covenant with the Trustees of the First Mortgage Bonds of this Company, to pay the principal of said Bonds, at maturity, in United States gold coin.

In accordance with this resolution, the President and Treasurer made the following

Covenant.

Know all Men by these Presents, *that Whereas*, the Union Pacific Railroad Company heretofore executed to EDWIN D. MORGAN, and OAKES AMES, Trustees, a certain Indenture of Mortgage bearing date the first day of November, one thousand eight hundred and sixty-five, mortgaging thereby the railroad of the said Company to the said Trustees to secure the payment of the said Company's First Mortgage Bonds, and the said Indenture of Mortgage was duly recorded; *And whereas*, the said Company have issued divers of the said first mortgage bonds, and intend hereafter to issue divers others of said first mortgage bonds mentioned in and provided for by the said indenture of mortgage; *And whereas*, by the tenor of said bonds the principal sum payable thereon at maturity is to be paid in lawful money of the United States; *Now*, in consideration of the premises, and of one dollar to the said Company in hand paid, the receipt whereof is hereby acknowledged, and for divers other good and valuable considerations, the said Company thereunto moving, the said Company hereby covenant and agree to and with the said EDWIN D. MORGAN and OAKES AMES, as Trustees, for the benefit of all who are or shall be holders of said bonds, and to and with the successors of said Trustees in the trust created by the said Indenture of Mortgage, that the principal of all the said First Mortgage Bonds being one thousand dollars each, as well such as have been issued hitherto as such as shall be issued hereafter, shall and will be paid by the said Company whensoever the same respectively become payable according to the tenor thereof, in the gold coin of the United States at par, that is to say, one thousand dollars of such coin for each of the said bonds.

In Witness whereof, the said Company have caused these presents to be sealed with their corporate seal, and to be subscribed by their President and Treasurer, this twelfth day of March, one thousand, eight hundred and sixty-eight.

Sealed and delivered in the presence of BENJAMIN F. HAM.

OLIVER AMES, *President.*
JOHN J. CISCO, *Treasurer.*

It will be noticed, that this covenant applies to all the First Mortgage Bonds of the Company without exception, including those that have been heretofore issued as well as those which may be issued hereafter. We now come to the first question which will be asked by every investor, viz.:

ARE THE BONDS SECURE?

Ans.: Congress has taken an especial care that the interests of the bondholders of this road shall be secured, that has never before been shown towards a similar enterprise. The Mortgage is made to Hon. E. D. MORGAN, U. S. Senator from New York, and Hon. OAKES AMES, Member of U. S. House of Representatives from Massachusetts, who alone can deliver the bonds to the Company, and who are responsible for their delivery in strict accordance with the terms of the law.

The President of the United States appoints Five Government

Directors who cannot be stockholders, who take part in the direction of all its affairs, and one of whom is to be on every Committee of the Company. It is the duty of these directors to see that all the business of the Company is properly managed, and to report the same to the Secretary of the Interior, who reports, through the President, to Congress.

The President of the United States also appoints three Commissioners to inspect the work as it progresses, in sections of twenty miles, to see that it is in all respects a first-class road, and that it is suitably provided with depots, stations, &c., and all the rolling stock necessary for its business. The U. S. Bonds are issued to the Company only as each section of twenty miles is accepted by the U. S. Commissioners, and the trustees of the first mortgage bondholders deliver the Company's own First Mortgage Bonds to the Company only on the same conditions, except that the Company are permitted to issue their bonds for one hundred miles in advance of the completed line, to cover a part of the cost of grading, &c.

To give every facility for the negotiation of the Company's First Mortgage Bonds, the Government makes its own bonds issued to the Company a *second lien* upon the road, with the understanding that the interest and a part if not all the principal may be paid by services rendered at a future day. Gen. SHERMAN says that "the Government could well afford to build the entire line if necessary, rather than it should remain unbuilt." It will be noticed that the Union Pacific Railroad is, in fact, a Government work, built under the supervision of Government officers, and to a large extent with Government money. *We may say without danger of contradiction that no bonds issued by any other company in this country, or, so far as we know, in the world, are made so secure by a responsible Government, as the First Mortgage Bonds of the Union Pacific Railroad Company.* They are not only a first mortgage upon a property that costs three times their amount, but upon a property of daily increasing value, and whose income is already more than three times their interest. First mortgage bonds, whose principal is so thoroughly secured, and whose interest is so liberal and so amply provided for, must be classed among the very safest and best securities. There are many persons who now prefer them to those of any state or nation, because they are secured upon a great and tangible *realty*, which can be in no way affected by political action.

There are 540 miles of the road now completed, and it is certain to be finished at an early day. The stockholders comprise men of great wealth and railroad experience, who have individually invested large amounts in the enterprise, and who are abundantly able to insure its success. Yet if the present Company *could* fail to complete the road, (which no one acquainted with their ample means can suppose possible,) the operation of the part now finished would more than pay the interest on the bonds, and the United States would be compelled to provide for the construction of the remainder for its own protection. It is universally admitted that when the road is finished it will be one of the most productive properties in the country. As the shortest line connecting Western Europe and Eastern Asia, and as the only line connecting the two grand divisions of a continent, the amount of its business will only be limited by its capacity. The future of such a road need not be *predicted*, for it can be *demonstrated*. It will not only be the most useful and the grandest, but we hazard nothing in asserting that it will be the most profitable work of modern times.

The question "*Are the Bonds secure?*" being answered, the next query must be,

WHAT ARE THEY WORTH AS AN INVESTMENT?

Ans.: Other conditions being the same, securities are valuable *according to their rate of interest.* The recent average quotations for U. S. 10-40 bonds, bearing only 5 per cent. gold interest, redeemable by the government in six years, have been 101 to 101½, and the U. S. 5-20's of '67, gold six per cents which may be redeemed in five years, have been at from 107 to 108. The best first mortgage six per cent. railroad *currency* bonds range at about par, and the seven per cents run to a considerable premium, while the Union Pacific First Mortgage Bonds are sure to pay six per cent. in gold, which, with the premium at 40, (where it has stood upon the average for about three years,) pay 8⅖ per cent.

Another and very important consideration in determining the value of these bonds is *the length of time they have to run.*

It is well known, that a long bond always commands a much higher price than a short one. With the U. S. 5-20's of '67, having five years to run, at from 7 to 8 per cent. premium, the 6's of '81, running thirteen years before maturity, bring 4 to 5 per cent. more. It is safe to assume, that during the next thirty years, the rate of interest in the United States will decline as it has done in the old countries of Europe, and we have a right to expect that such six per cent. securities as these will be held at as high a premium as those of this Government, which, in 1857, were bought in at from 20 to 23 per cent. above par.

There is no doubt that the Union Pacific Bonds will become a favorite investment abroad, for although the Company have made no effort to sell them, except at home, considerable amounts have been voluntarily taken on foreign account, and it is probable, that as soon as the road is completed, a very large proportion of the whole issue will be taken out of the country.

It should be remembered, that the whole issue of these bonds will be only about thirty million dollars, of which over twelve millions have already been sold. The amount to be offered during the current year will not be more than ten to twelve millions, and while subscriptions are now received at par, it is expected that, with a favorable money market, the price will be advanced to a premium at an early day.

In addition to their safety and profit, these bonds offer every convenience of a convertible investment. The gold coupons will be cashed by bankers in any part of the country, and the bonds themselves are taken as security for loans at the lowest current rates.

Full particulars in relation to terms, agents, and means of subscribing may be found in the advertisement on the last page of the cover.

NEW YORK, April 2, 1868.

JOHN J. CISCO, TREASURER,
Union Pacific Railroad Company.

www.ingramcontent.com/pod-product-compliance
Lightning Source LLC
LaVergne TN
LVHW011122110826
845150LV00008B/2229

* 9 7 8 1 4 1 8 1 9 5 3 6 6 *